The Story of Beautiful Jim Key

The Story of Beautiful Jim Key

The Arabian Hambletonian Educated Horse

——*Valued at $100,000.00*——

HE
eads
'rites
pells
ounts
'gures
hanges
oney
ells
ime
ses a
a s h
egister
c., etc.

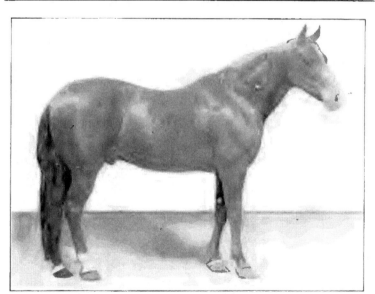

The Most Wonderful Horse in all the world

OFFICES GODDARD BUILDING
19 MILK STREET

Boston, Oct. 22nd., *1901*

Mr. Albert R. Rogers,

My Dear Sir;-

It gives me great pleasure to inform you that you and Dr. William Key and beautiful "Jim Key" have been elected Honorary Members of the "Parent American Band of Mercy", whose branches now number, in our own and other countries, probably between two and three millions members.

Geo T. Angell

President of the American Humane Education Society, the Massachusetts Society for the Prevention of Cruelty to Animals, and the Parent American Band of Mercy.

TAKING A SILVER DOLLAR OUT OF A GLASS JAR OF WATER

JIM KEY'S BUILDING AT THE EXPORT EXPOSITION, PHILADELPHIA.

P R E F A C E.

How was Beautiful Jim Key taught ? How did his teacher, Dr. Key, come to notice the extra intelligence this horse possessed? What breed is he? And a dozen similar questions are asked so often, that the writer has tried to give in the following pages, the answers to them all. The beautiful and touching story is related, of the devotion of the typical old Uncle Tom, "Dr. Wm. Key," to his master during the civil war, and the romantic story of the stealing from Sheik Ahemid, in Arabia, of the famous Lauretta, known as the Mother of Horses, and who was the dam of Beautiful Jim Key.

The illustrations cover Beautiful Jim Key's principal acts.

BEAUTIFUL, JIM KEY.
The Most Intelligent Horse in the World.

CHANGING MONEY.

The romantic story of Lauretta, the Arabian dam of Jim Key.

The Queen of Horses.

A number of years ago, amidst the Nesaen pastures of Persia, the great Sheik Ahemid, a powerful ruler, envied and admired by all, ruled in love and firmness o'er his tribe, that stretched into far off Arabian sands. For was there not in his dowar (tented home) the Queen of all Arabian horses, the fair Lauretta, with a lineage carefully kept on tablets of ivory that reached back to the broods of Pharaoh, comrades, friends of the tented tribes whom long association, love and kindness had nearly brought up to their own plane, and when to their animal instincts had been added wits and a reasoning sense, they feel and know all of ambition, love and hate.

In every black tent down to the Arkaba and to the ocean, and across to the Euphrates and beyond to the sea of the Scynthians, the renown of Lauretta, the worshipped of all, was the daily talk, and for her health and safety their daily Allahs.

This evening the good Sheik's heart was heavy and anger knitted the furrows deeper in his brow. A trusted stranger had stolen the Mother Queen of Horses, Lauretta, and though a full moon had passed, no word yet had been heard from his beloved, and all over Arabia mutterings of anger were heard, even some saying he himself had sold her, and the false story was going on the winds of the evening.

The Arabian's Story.

Clapping his hands thrice, the heavy curtains parted, and there entered with silent, gliding steps his head servant, Mohammed. "Well, son of the desert, repeat thou the tale, aye, repeat it word for word, and by my beard, if thou contradict thyself but once," and his eyes blazed fire, but stopping himself, he said, "go on."

"'Twas but a moon ago the stranger came," Mohammed recited, "came with tablets from the great Lallah, and thou entertained him as befitting a Sheik, though he was light of hair, oil was his tongue, flattery caused thou to trust him. To show him thy loved ones, to let him try their paces, even ride Lauretta, our famed Queen." At the name the Sheik bounded to his feet, rage shot lightning from his eyes, with clenched hands he grasped his spear, and then as quickly seating himself, he moaned, "my beautiful, my beautiful." Then one evening he told you the tale—a great Sheik in far off England who had great power and whose desire was to purchase our beautiful Lauretta—the Mother of Horses—who would give the price, a thousand horses. Ah! thy rage I will remember ever—'sell Lauretta, my Queen, sell the Mother of all Horses, to whom a million allahs are said—pluck out mine eyes, but part not I with my beautiful, raised here in my tented dowar—but go on.'

"The morning came, and when Rama came to bring drink to the beloved ones, there was no Lauretta, but in the side of the cloth a great cut. I awoke you, O Master, and though a thousand of your tried horsemen galloped madly over the desert sand, no signs of the Mother was found. The shifting sands, blown with every breeze, hid her tracks—and the stranger gone."

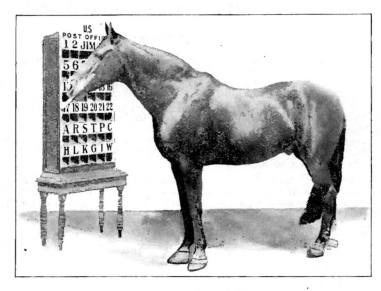

ACTING POSTMASTER.

4

Lauretta Stolen.

'Twas early dawn when Jack Randall, the emissary of the greatest of all showmen, awoke. Bribes, entreaties, even her weight in gold, had failed to make the good Sheik sell Lauretta. Jack awoke with a start, for he had lain awake half the night scheming—dare he do it? 'Twould mean death, a terrible death, at the hands of the infuriated Arabs if he was caught; but who could catch Lauretta? Was she not as swift as the very winds? Peeping out of his tent the stars were shining; the heavy breathing of the men sent a shiver through him. He slowly crept out; 'twas but a hundred yards to the tent where Lauretta and Philis, and Ectes and Ranus, the kingly four, were, but how to get in it, for two Arabs slept at its entrance. So, gliding in the semi-darkness, he came to the back of the tent made of skins; his big knife slit it as high as he could reach on tip-toe. 'Twas a moment that made his hair turn gray, but there at the very place stood Lauretta, her trappings on a post near her. No hesitation now; 'twas a lifetime in the minute it took to sling a bridle on her noble head and lead her out. Cautiously, with silent tread, in the sand he led her, and then bounding on her back glided as if she had wings, out in the desert. No saddle cloth had he, but like a Centaur he sat astride, and urged her on and on, faster and faster, for well he knew that seconds meant for him life and gold.

A Sensation in Europe.

"What a tremendous sensation a horse can make," said a gray-haired diplomat one day in Parliament. "Here is the gray Arabian mare that is drawing such crowds at the circus because she was known as the Queen of Arabian Horses, causing us no end of annoyance by the fanatics of Arabia because they say she was stolen; others say that Sheik Ahemid sold her, and his numerous followers have deserted him, and all because of one gray mare. And Lauretta, the once proud Queen of the desert, now the slave of a circus owner, though the greatest in the land, to be exhibited to the tens of thousands of the curious."

Bought by Dr. Wm. Key.

Through carelessness and unkind treatment she broke down, and was taken to America and sold again to a smaller circus, that after a short life became stranded in the South, at Cupola, Miss. To get away the owners sold at auction some of their horses, and a colored man, well known as a Veterinary, in Shelbyville, Tenn., Dr. Wm. Key, bought her for $40.00, though it is stated she cost $50,000 when first purchased.

Lauretta fell into kind and able hands, for Dr. Key was celebrated throughout the Southland for both his marvellous skill and kindness in the treatment of horses, and though it took nearly a year of the most careful attention, the good Doctor, for so he is best known, cured her.

DR. WM. KEY.

PROGRAM.

The audience are requested to ask questions. Please speak distinctly to the horse and he will respond promptly. A hint—he enjoys applause.

1. He opens school. Rings the bell for school to open.
2. Jim picks out any letter, playing card or number asked for.
3. Jim shows his proficiency in figuring, adding, multiplying, dividing and subtracting in any numbers below thirty.
4. He spells any ordinary name asked him.
5. He reads and writes.
6. He goes to the post-office, gets the mail from any box requested, and files the letter in a regular letter file, under any name asked him.
7. Jim distinguishes various pieces of money, and goes to a cash register and rings up any amount asked for, bringing the correct change.
8. Distinguishes colors and flags, and tells the time.
9. Gives quotations from the Bible, where the horse is mentioned, giving chapter and verse.
10. Uses the telephone.
11. Jim takes a silver dollar from the bottom of a glass jar filled with water, without drinking a drop. (Considered one of the greatest feats ever performed by an animal.)
12. Jim offered for sale. Not wanting to leave, he goes lame. Well again. (One of his most amusing and laughable feats.)

6

READING.

How Beautiful Jim Key was taught, by Dr. William Key.

Finely Bred.

"For nearly a year after Jim was foaled I had no hope of him. Knowing he was the finest bred horse in the country, I was very anxious to see what he would turn out, for Lauretta, his dam, was the smartest horse I had ever seen, and his sire, Tennessee Volunteer— well, he couldn't be beat. But Jim pretty near done broke my heart, for he was the most spingled, shank-legged animal I ever did see. There was an old, no-account, bow-legged nigger named Jim that lived near me, and I named Jim after him, though I had some very fine Bible names picked out; but I took mighty fine care of Jim, and before long, his legs began to straighten out. He was a knowing colt, I tell you. He just lived in my house and would follow me around like a dog. He wanted to know what everything was, and I commenced to teach him simple things. One of the first things he learned, and I didn't teach it to him, either, was to unfasten the gate and let himself out in the road.

7

He Began Early.

"I began to teach him when he was one year old. First, I taught him to lie down and roll, and soon after that to give symptoms of bots and colic, because I was then in the medicine business. Next he learned to make-believe he was lame and act as though he were suffering with different kinds of troubles, the general symptoms of which he would reproduce. I had him learn to bring me different things and then to learn different colors. The hardest thing I had to teach him was to learn how to eat sugar. I tried every way, and had it tied to the bridle, but Jim would always spit it out. One day I saw him eating apples in the orchard, and I got the idea that if I put a piece of sugar in an apple he would eat it. I fixed an apple and then watched Jim. When he picked it up and munched it I thought he would go crazy with satisfaction and delight. I at once tried the sugar alone, but it was no use. He had taken a grudge against raw sugar, although he would take it with an apple coating. I worked with him for six months before I succeeded. I had to cover the apple with sugar and he would eat both with great relish. I gradually reduced the quantity of apple over the sugar, and then he would have a piece of apple laid over a piece of sugar in my hand, and when he would reach for the apple he would get the sugar. In this way he soon learned that sugar was sugar and apple was apple.

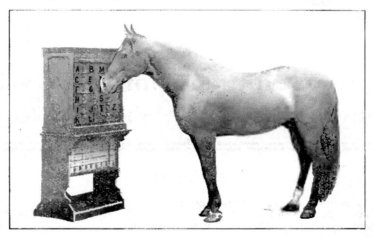

FILING LETTERS.

The Learning of the Alphabet.

"The learning of the alphabet was the work that required the most patience. I had to keep at it all the time for years. When I began I had in my mind only to teach Jim to pick out the letter A. I got some cards with the letter A on it, and then put sugar on the card. This was, of course, after Jim had grown to have a passion for sugar, which he has never lost. I would say to him, 'A, A, A,' and while I was doing this I would let nobody in the stable, and I would keep him away from other horses. I said 'A' a good many times, and Jim used up many cards, as he would lick the cards so much.

Bringing Letters.

"Finally I got a piece of tin with the letter painted on it. It took months and months, a half year, before I was satisfied that he would know the letter A when he would see it. When I had this done I thought that if Jim could only be made to bring the card to me I would have just what I wanted. I at once began to train him for this end. I began with a piece of apple in a handkerchief. I would let him get the end in his jaw and then I would try to draw it away from him. Finally I would have a piece of apple in my hand, and hold out the handkerchief to him, and then give him the apple. He learned that he was being rewarded, and I soon had him tugging at the card and then bringing it to me. Then I thought that I had my fortune made when one day I happened to think if the horse knew A when he saw it he could be taught the entire alphabet, and in this I was right.

Taught to Say Yes.

"My wife used to tell me to let the horse alone and come out of the stable, for she knew that I would go crazy over Jim, but it came around so that she got very fond of Jim, and was soon very much attached to him. One day she happened to go into the stable while eating an apple, and she said, 'Jim, do you want a piece of apple?' He bowed his head up and down. The next thing I heard was my wife calling out, 'Doctor, doctor, the horse can say yes.' I went in, but Jim would not say it to me. I went out and watched and saw him do it for my wife. From that day she fell in love with him, and would always reward him with apples or sugar whenever he would do what she asked of him. The way Jim learned to open and close the desk drawers was this: I had put some apples in a drawer that had a string attached to it. Later on I returned and all the apples were gone. I suspected some boys that were about the place, and when I put some more apples in the drawer they, too, disappeared, and then I watched and soon found that Jim was stealing my apples. He had been watching me, and soon began imitating me.

Figuring.

"From that time on my work was comparatively easy. I taught him to count, and then to figure. This took years, but I kept at it—day after day—until now he knows up to thirty. Jim likes writing and quickly learns names printed on card board. I believe he knows every word I say to him, and sometimes it seems to me all I've got to do is to think a thing and he knows it. Yes, some say it's hypnotism and that kind of thing—but I don't know anything about that, but I do know Jim knows and does what I ask him to do. It was just kindness, mere kindness, and no more. Now I am spending all my time teaching him the places and quotations where the horse is mentioned in the Bible, for horses were mighty prominent animals then. The Prophets had visions of them. John says he looked up and beheld a white horse in heaven, and what Jim wants to know is, if there are white horses in heaven, why can't a good bay horse go there also?

9

He Travels in a Private Car, Dr. Key His Bed=Fellow.

Always Watched.

"Beautiful Jim Key always travels in a palace car, although he dislikes the jarring of travel, and refuses to lay down while on the road, because the bumping of stops and starts of the train would jar him rudely. When he makes a long journey he is granted a stop-over at a half-way point in order that he may enjoy the comforts of a box stall and obtain his night's rest.

"When at home or stabling in some city where he is on exhibition, Jim Key has his faithful old valet for his stall mate. The Doctor places his cot in the stall with his pet, and the two sleep together 365 nights of the year. During the working hours Jim is never unattended. Either the Doctor, who trained him, or a groom is constantly by his side, and he could not be given more constant care and attention were he the fleetest racer in the world on the eve of the most important Derby of the turf. Even his grain and hay, though the choicest quality that can be bought, is examined very closely to see that no impurities are in it.

What He Drinks.

"His drinking water is not from the common hydrant, but is the purest spring water that can be secured; often bottled water is secured for him. He drinks only water from which all the impurities have been filtered.

"Every morning he has his gallop, and comes in reeking with perspiration to receive an hour's rubbing and combing until his coat fairly shines, and is then in fine condition for his daily work.

"Jim is a splendid saddle horse and has led many big parades. His beautiful arched neck and the graceful curves of his body and long, sweeping tail make a beautiful picture, as he keeps step to the music, though prancing and fairly dancing. At the New Orleans Horse Show and many others where he has been on exhibition, he has taken all the blue ribbons in several classes.

He Appreciates Applause.

"In breeding he is Arabian and Hambletonian, as elsewhere related. His height is 16 hands; mahogany bay; he is 11 years of age (June, 1901). Never has been sick; always takes especial delight in his work; seems eager to learn, and no actor ever was prouder of making a great hit than is Jim when playing before a large house that show their appreciation of him by their applause. His appreciation of applause is one of the most human traits he has, and sometimes when he has a small audience he does not act as quickly and really seems to feel as if he was not being appreciated.

"Jim understands what one is saying. When he is praised his head goes up so as to say, 'What horse is as smart as I?'

SPELLING.

Valued at $100,000.
His New Owner.

First Exhibited.

While at the Nashville Exposition, Mr. A. R. Rogers, a business man of New York, saw for the first time this marvellous, intelligent animal. Being very greatly interested in humane societies, and a great lover of horses in particular, he purchased from Dr. Key for $10,000 this beautiful animal, but Dr. Key put in the contract a clause to this effect: I am always to be Jim Key's groom and teacher," for he would not part with his pet. So North went Jim and Dr. Key to Mr. Rogers' beautiful country home in the Oranges, a suburb of New York, and here for a year Jim was given his finishing touches before he was ever put on public exhibition. Since that time many offers have been made to buy Jim, one party offering $60,000, but Jim Key is not for sale at any price, for not only does he earn more money than any other horse, but he is a missionary.

Teaches People to be Kind to Animals.

Last year at his performances over 185,000 boys and girls promised him to always be kind to animals, and thousands of adults after seeing his remarkable performance have gone away with the same resolve in their hearts.

BRINGING LETTERS.

Sketch of Dr. Wm. Key's Life.

Wm. Key was born in Winchester, Tenn., sixty-five years ago, and was named after his master, John W. Key, a well-known planter of Shelbyville, Tenn. In his early years he had a great fondness for the animals. Ever kind to them, and many a poor dog or a worried cat was he the defender of on the old plantation. They tell a story that when Bill Key, as he was called, was six years old, he had a rooster and a yellow dog that would do wonderful things. His entry into the barnyard was the signal for a general commotion, for all the animals, big and little, seemed to recognize in him a friend. If a colt was to be broken Bill was sent for by the neighbors for miles around, for he did it by kindness. He would take the wild, frightened colt up to his master's farm, and in a week's time by his gentle, patient care would return him ready to ride or drive. So remarkable was his success with balking and kicking mules, in which he took a special pride, that the "colored population" used to say he bewitched them. Uncle Bill is a mulatto and a veterinary surgeon. Born a slave, he was one of those fortunate men who had a kind master, and when the war clouds began to hover over the Southland and his master's sons left home to defend their cause, Uncle Bill went with them "to look after his young masters," as he states.

"They just went with Gen. Palmer's at Murfreesborough, Tenn. Their company was called the Festerville Guards, Captain Webb."

Asked why he went into the army instead of seeking his freedom, he said: "I loved my young marsters. I was afraid they would get killed or not have anything to eat, so I went with them." "And did you keep them from being killed?" the reporter asked him. "Yes, sir. We was at Fort Donaldson, Tenn., and when the Yankees captured us I stole them out of prison and took them into the rebel lines."

12

Fort Bill.

It was at Fort Donaldson that he built his famous fort called by the soldiers Fort Bill—a small place dug in the ground and covered with logs to keep the bullets out; where he would seek cover, he said, when they began to shoot, and where he would try and coax his young marsters. When Fort Donaldson surrendered in the night Bill tole out and found a place unguarded and took his young masters out with important papers, and they escaped. They then joined Gen. Forest, acting as scouts and guides. After the Stone river battle Bill undertook to get another darkey through the lines, but was caught by the guard, the Sixth Indiana Regiment, and quickly thrust into prison as a spy. He says, "I told the Yanks I was tired of the rebels and wanted to be free; but they called in some men who were Union men, that lived at my home, and they told the officers I was the worst rebel in the South, and to hold me till they caught my young master, A. W. Key, and hang us both together.

"I staid in that prison six weeks, when one day Gen. Naglee stated he wanted a cook, and some one who knew me told him I was the best cook in the country, so he and Capt Prather both came and wanted me. I liked the looks of Capt. Prather, and I knew he was a great poker-player, and I had never found a man that could beat me, so I went with Capt. Prather and in six weeks I owned everything he had; he owed me over a thousand dollars. He gave me a pass to go home for the debt.

"At the battle of Shiloh I was with my young master again, and I tried to shoot him in the calve of the leg so that he would not have to fight any more, but he kept too close a watch on me.

Went to Get $100,000.

"The second time the Yanks caught me I went into their lines to get $500,000 in Confederate money. A man who knew me offered me $100,000 in Confederate money if I would go to a certain store which a Union man kept and bring back the money that was hid there. I didn't like this job, but there was so much money in it that one night I stole out by the camp, and when I had got in the town the first man I met was my worst enemy.

In a Slave Driver's Grasp.

"He was a slave-driver, and had tried to buy me; and when I persuaded my master not to sell me he swore he would get me some day and lick the blood out of me. Well, he clapped me into prison and told me he would have me hung before daylight; and he would, but a lawyer, W. H. Wiseman, who knew me, and that I had money, said if I would give him $1,000 he would get me off. I had the money in my shoe, sewed between the soles.

"My case was put off time and time again by this lawyer, and one day the inspector said he wanted a good whitewasher. I told him that was my regular business, and that my brushes were at a certain store in town. He sent me there with a guard. I went behind the counter and pulled off the sole of my shoe and gave the money to a lady who run the store, and she gave it to Lawyer Wiseman. The next day the rebels raided and captured the place, and I was let go and my money was gone too.

13

Went into the Medicine Business.

"I had a liniment which I called 'Keystone Liniment,' and everybody wanted it, so that started me into the medicine business. I used to travel around the country with a minstrel band to attract a crowd, and then sell my medicine. One day a man told me that a circus was going to sell out. I bought some of their horses. Lauretta, the Arabian mother of Jim, was one of them."

A few years later Beautiful Jim Key was foaled, and the interesting story of the years of patient work in teaching him is told elsewhere.

Few men have seen as much varied life as has Dr. Key, and few men have done as much good. It is said that the doctor is worth close onto a hundred thousand dollars, but his love for Jim is so strong that he prefers to travel around with him rather than live in ease.

Mr. Rogers, who bought Jim, and pays Dr. Key a large salary, says he is the most faithful man he ever met. "I would trust him with all I have as I would myself."

The years of patience it took to teach this wonderful horse are only to be equalled by the horse's nearly human intelligence. It has been said that Beautiful Jim Key is a missionary to his kind. Surely Dr. Key has proven that kindness and patience will accomplish much more than force. He even sleeps by the horse, whose life is so wrapped in his own, and in whom he takes such a pride.

Mayor Dudley of Nashville relates the following incident in regard to Dr. Wm. Key when he was exhibiting Jim Key at Sam Jones' Tabernacle in Nashville. It is a clipping from the Nashville American:

While looking over a list of appointments which Mayor Dudley has ahead, and which will consequently have to be broken, he came across one in which he was down for a speech at the opening performance Monday of Jim Key, the celebrated horse which will be exhibited at the Tabernacle under the auspices of the local Humane Society.

Pays His Master's Mortgage.

"I regret very much that I cannot fill that engagement," said Mayor Dudley to the reporter today, "but I have written Gov. McMillin and asked him to take my place on the programme.

Outside of the good accomplished by the exhibition, presenting as it does an object lesson of what kindness will do when directed toward animals," continued the Mayor, "a feeling of sentiment actuates me. You may not know it, but Dr. Jim Key, the colored man who trained the horse and who still has him in charge, and I were boys together in Bedford County. The Doctor was a slave then and his master ran a tanyard about four miles from my father's home. I often went to the tanyard and there met Dr. Key, as he afterward became known. He was always respectful and gentlemanly, and I learned to like the little fellow.

"At the breaking out of the war his young master joined the Confederate army, and Jim went with him, remaining throughout the period of hostilities. Upon returning home the tanyard and almost everything else belonging to the family was found destroyed. Jim went to work, however, and in a few years he succeeded in paying off a mortgage of $5,000 which hung over his master's home. So you can see why I feel kindly disposed toward Jim and any enterprise with which he is connected. I hope the people of Nashville will give the performances the support which they so richly deserve," concluded the Mayor.

Some of Beautiful Jim Key's Great Successes.

Jim has exhibited in Boston, Cincinnati, Nashville (2), Atlanta, Birmingham, Chattanooga, New Orleans (2), Philadelphia (3), Pittsburg (2), Atlantic City (2), Trenton, and Reading, besides many of the big State Fairs, and his success has been phenomenal. The following few examples illustrate his earning powers, for no single attraction has ever taken in half the money that Jim Key has, and it is no uncommon sight to see hundreds waiting to get into his place of exhibition—as if he was some famous actor.

THREE PERFORMANCES—Sam Jones Tabernacle, Nashville, Tenn. Attendance, 17,610.

THREE WEEKS—New Orleans Exposition. Receipts, $5,211.50.

ONE WEEK—Muncie Street Fair. Receipts, $1,847.

TEN WEEKS—Riverview Park, Baltimore "The greatest drawing card and money maker we ever had. Our Casino packed five times a day. The longest run of any attraction ever in Baltimore. The talk of the city." JAMES L. KERNAN, Manager.

SEVEN WEEKS—Export Exposition, Philadelphia. Receipts, $20,-612.90. "According to the records of this department there were 173,260 tickets of admissions sold to visitors of the Educated Horse, beautiful Jim Key, resulting in the sum of $20,612.90. This attraction proved to be the best patronized of the numerous shows on our midway."
W. E. CASH, Chief Deputy of Concessions.

15

SIX WEEKS—Pittsburgh Exposition. Receipts, $7,000. Two years previous he was there as a free attraction. Three weeks the next year, same place. Receipts, $5,000.

FOUR WEEKS—Boston Food Fair. The greatest drawing card, and charging an extra admission his receipts were $5,000.

Copies For Sale. Price 25 Cents.
A. R. ROGERS, 75 Maiden Lane, New York City.

Season 1901,
Young's Ocean Pier, Atlantic City.

"I have never had such a drawing card on my pier before; during our large attendance at Easter time, over 80 per cent. of the thousands who thronged my pier paid an extra admission to see Jim Key."

JOHN L. YOUNG.

Jim Key's phenomenal record at Young's Ocean Pier, Atlantic City, opening in their Theatre March 17th, and staying until Sept. 1st, playing daily except Sunday to thousands of delighted, astonished people, many coming and coming again to see him, is a record unequalled by any other show or company.

Mr. A. R. Rogers,

South Orange,

N. J.,

BROOKLINE, MASS.   13th Nov.,   1900

Dear Mr. Rogers,

It gives me pleasure to inform you that at the annual convention of the American Humane Association recently held at Pittsburgh, Pa., "Beautiful Jim Key" was elected an honorary member of the Association. I think this is the first instance on record of such an act on the part of our organization. It was an expression of our appreciation of the intelligence of the horse, the kindness of his trainer and the generosity of his owner.

Very sincerely yours,

Francis H Rowley

Secretary

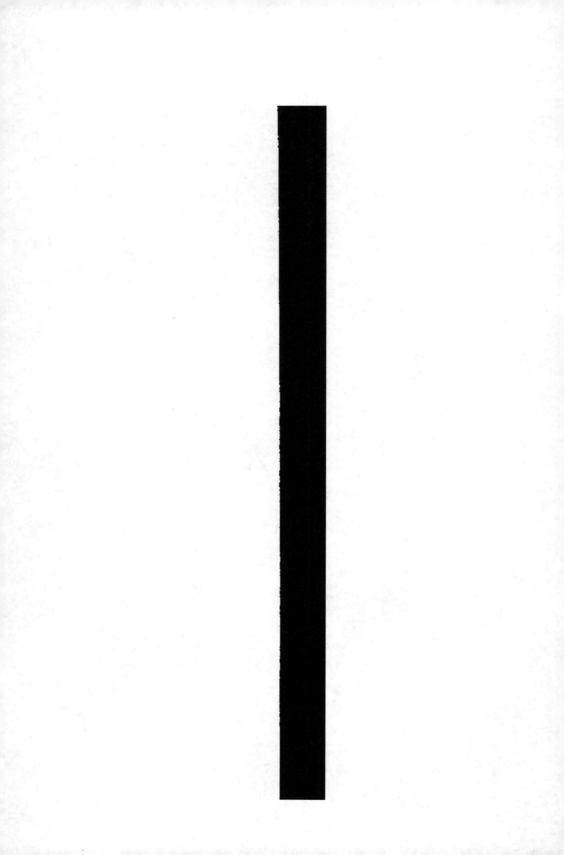

CPSIA information can be obtained
at www.ICGtesting.com
Printed in the USA
BVHW042058180721
612152BV00004B/341